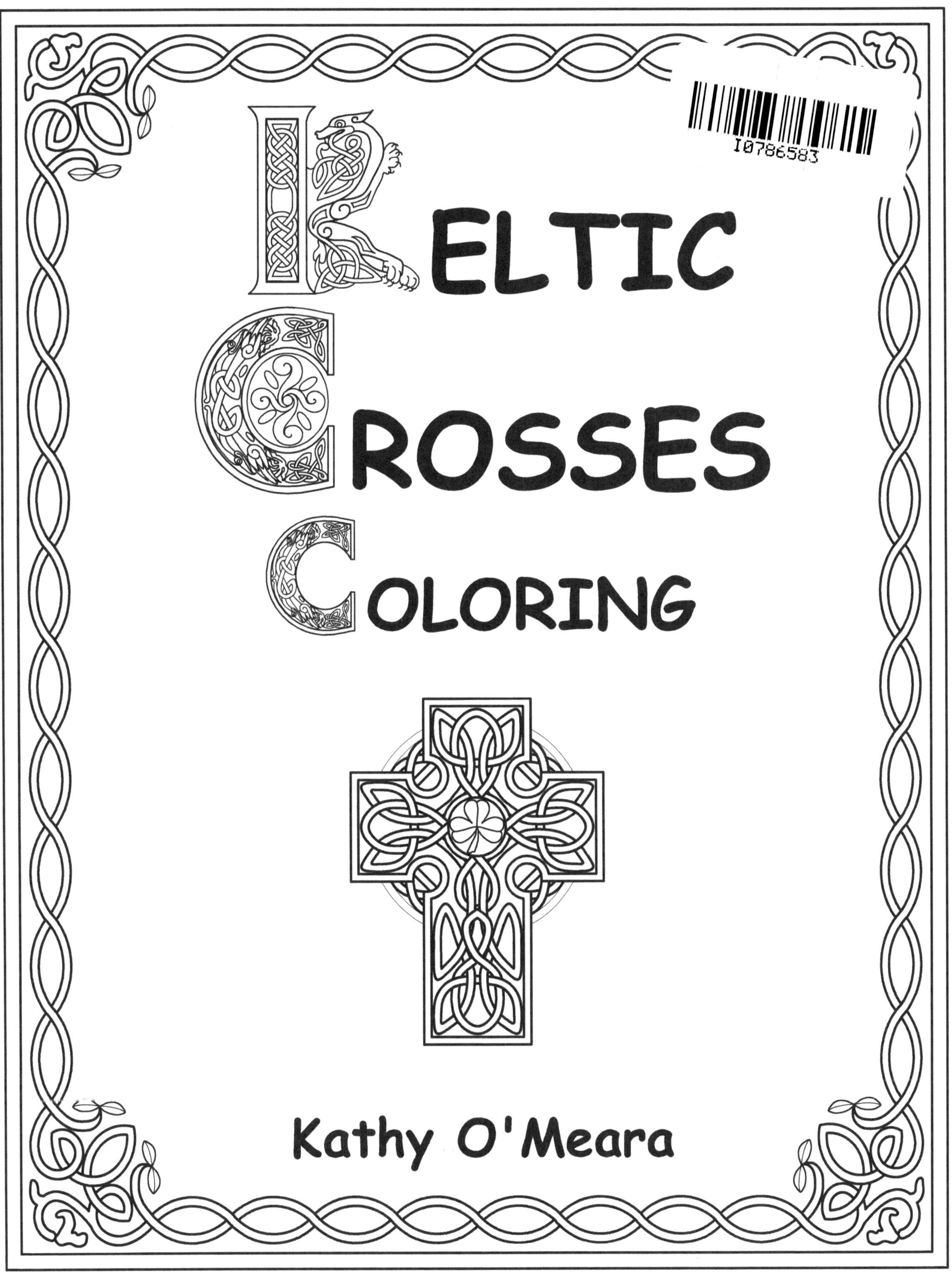

KELTIC
CROSSES
COLORING
Kathy O'Meara

Perelandra
Design

This book is dedicated
to my Father, Frank O'Meara,
and C.S. Lewis; with both I share
my Irish Heritage and my Christian Faith.

International Standard Book Number

ISBN-13: 978-1717578433
ISBN-10: 1717578438